Helping Children See Jesus

ISBN: 978-1-64104-056-3

Law and Liberty
*New Testament Volume 28:
Galatians Part 3*

Author: Marilyn P. Habecker
Illustrator: Frances H. Hertzler
Colorization courtesy of Good Life Ministries
Typesetting and Layout: Patricia Pope

© 2019 Bible Visuals International
PO Box 153, Akron, PA 17501-0153
Phone: (717) 859-1131
www.biblevisuals.org

All rights reserved. No part of this publication may be reproduced, stored in a retrieval system or transmitted in any form by any means, electronic, mechanical, photocopy, recording or otherwise, without the prior permission of the publisher, except as provided by USA copyright law.

RELATED ITEMS

To access related items (such as activities, memory verse posters and translated texts) please visit our web store at www.biblevisuals.org and enter 1028 at the top right of the web page. You may need to reduce the zoom setting to get the search box.

FREE TEXT DOWNLOAD

To obtain a FREE printable copy of the English teaching text (PDF format) under Product Format, please scroll down and select Extra–PDF Teacher Text Download. Then under Language select English before clicking the ADD TO CART button to place in your shopping cart. Other languages are available at an additional cost from the Language menu. When checking out, use coupon code XTACSV17 at checkout and click on Apply Coupon to receive the discount on the English text.

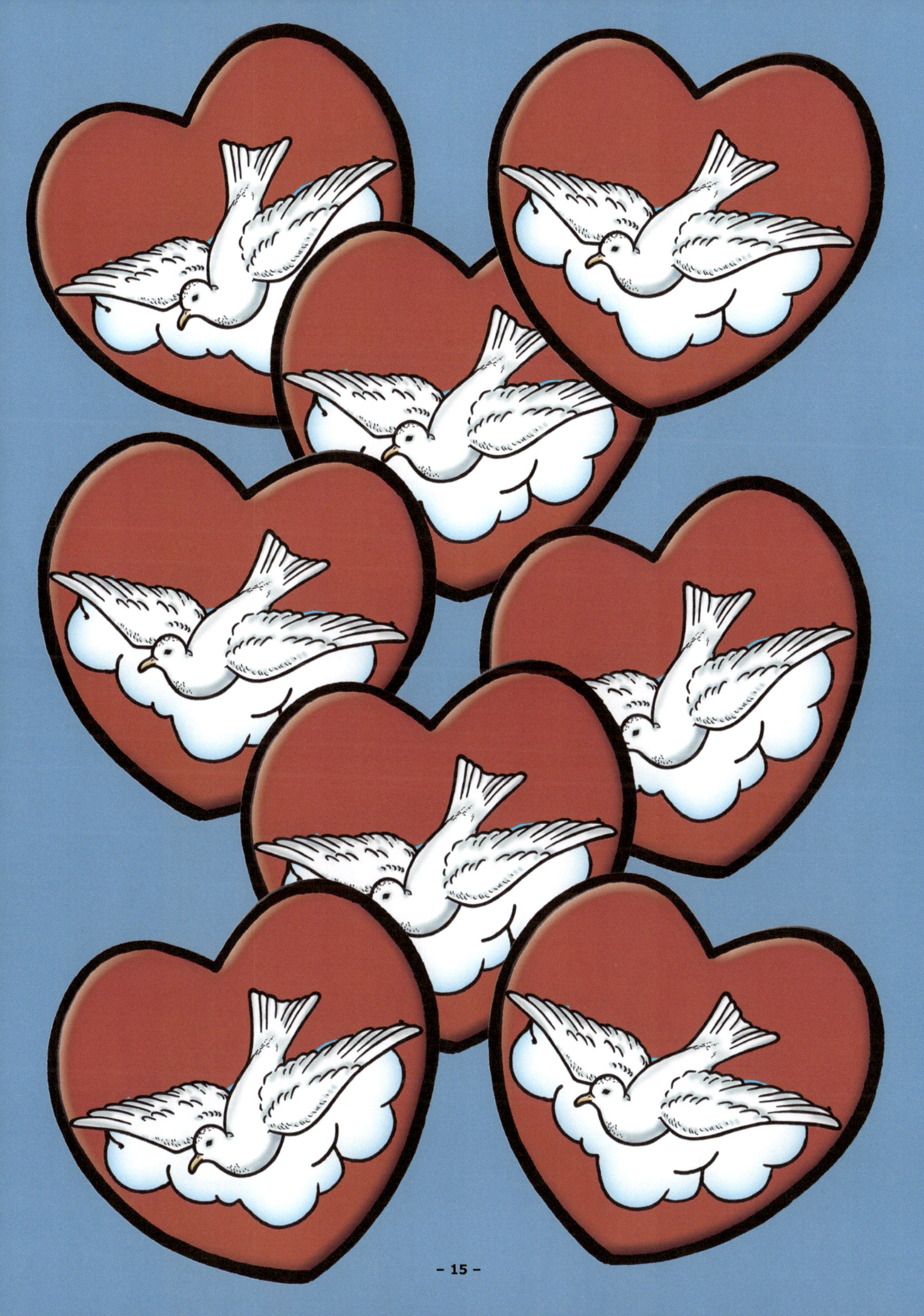

Walk in the Spirit, and ye shall not fulfil the lust of the flesh. Galatians 5:16

Lesson 1
CHRISTIAN LIBERTY

Scripture to be studied: Galatians 5:1-14

The *aim* of the lesson: To challenge students to become love slaves of Jesus Christ.

What your students should *know*: Christian liberty is freedom to serve the Lord by helping others.

What your students should *feel*: Gratitude to God for the liberty He gives.

What your students should *do*: Each day this week, out of pure love for God and His Son, do something that will help either a weak Christian or one who is not a Christian.

Lesson outline (for teacher's and students' notebooks):

1. Law is slavery, (Galatians 5:1b-4).
2. Liberty is freedom, (Galatians 5:1).
3. Liberty is governed by love, (Galatians 5:6, 13).
4. Liberty results in service, (Galatians 5:13b).

The verse to be memorized:

Walk in the Spirit, and ye shall not fulfil the lust of the flesh. (Galatians 5:16)

> **NOTE TO THE TEACHER**
>
> In the book of Galatians, Paul explains that the Galatian believers fell from their high position in God's grace to the level of trying to earn salvation. As a result they were bound like slaves, unable to enjoy the freedom which Christ gives His own. In the light of what he has taught in the four opening chapters of the book, Paul uses the last two chapters to discuss Christian liberty and the correct way to practice it. This series, therefore, is extremely practical and deserves serious study.

THE LESSON

Most people today are treated kindly by their masters (employers). This was not always so. In early Bible times servants were often slaves. If they failed to do what their masters required, they were beaten like animals. (See Exodus 1:11; 3:7; 5:6, 10, 13-14.) When the Israelites were the Egyptian's slaves, they cried to God to be set free. They hated their slavery.

God answered them saying, "I have heard your groanings . . . . I will bring you out from slavery . . . . I will make you free. (See Exodus 6:5-7.) In due time God kept His promise and His people were set free. That was certainly a wonderful day.

The Galatians, too, were once slaves, slaves to the false gods which they worshiped. Their idol worship filled them with fear. Then Paul preached the Gospel of salvation to them. They received it gladly, found peace and happiness through trusting in the Saviour, and were free from their slavish idol worship.

1. LAW IS SLAVERY
Galatians 5:1b-4

Show Illustration #1

For a while the Galatians enjoyed God's saving grace. (*Teacher:* Point to figure on top line.) Then some other teachers taught them that receiving Christ as Saviour was not enough. If they wanted to be certain of eternal life, they would also have to observe special days and perform rituals contained in the Jewish law. Unfortunately, the Galatians accepted this false teaching.

So Paul wrote them, "Do not allow yourselves to be bound like slaves. You used to be slaves to sin. Now you are making yourselves slaves to the law. You have fallen down from the heights of grace." (See Galatians 5:1-4.)

Instead of enjoying God's gift of free salvation, the Galatians were making slaves of themselves by trying to follow part of the law. (*Teacher:* Point to chained figure on bottom line.)

Have you made the same mistake as the Galatians? You may have thought, I have been saved by God's grace through faith in Jesus Christ. Now I must do or not do certain things if I am to be KEPT saved. The result is that you're never certain that you've done enough right things or that you've done too many wrong things. And you're never sure of your salvation. Not being sure of your salvation is the worst kind of slavery. Like oxen in a yoke, you are in bondage (Galatians 5:1). You are not free.

2. LIBERTY IS FREEDOM
Galatians 5:1

Paul says to you (as he said to the Galatians), "Because Christ has set you free, stand fast in that liberty . . . . for you have been called unto liberty." (See Galatians 5:1, 13.) Liberty is being free from the chains of slavery.

Show Illustration #2

When the Lord Jesus died on the cross, He was crucified between two thieves. One spoke hateful words to Jesus. The other said to the first thief, "Aren't you afraid of God, even when you are dying? We deserve to die. But this Man has not done one wrong thing." Turning to Jesus he said, "Lord, remember me when You come into Your Kingdom." Immediately the Lord Jesus promised the second thief, "Today you will be with Me in a place of blessing." (See Luke 23:39-43.)

Because that thief placed his trust in the Lord Jesus Christ, he was set free from the kingdom of darkness. (See Colossians 1:13.) He had the promise of being with the Lord forever in His marvelous light. (See 1 Peter 2:9.) He did nothing to earn his freedom. The Lord Jesus did it all. In the same way, Christ Jesus will set you free if you trust in Him. He will set you free from the darkness of sin and also from Jewish laws and customs. This is liberty which God wants you to enjoy.

Paul didn't mean that the Galatians were free to do anything they wanted to do after they were saved. That's why he explained, "You are chosen to be free…live this free life by loving and serving others." (See Galatians 5:13.) That is, because God chose to set them free from sin, they were free to love and serve others. Do you have this freedom?

3. LIBERTY IS GOVERNED BY LOVE
Galatians 5:6, 13

Show Illustration #3

In Paul's first letter to the Corinthians (8:1-13), he explained how this love freedom works. In those days practically all the meats that were sold in the Corinthian markets had already been dedicated to idols. The Christians hesitated to eat such meats. They were afraid that others might get the impression that they approved of idol worship. They knew this would dishonor the Lord.

Paul taught them that an idol is nothing (1 Corinthians 8:4). There is only the one true and living God of Heaven. Since an idol is nothing, the meat had been offered to nothing. Therefore it was all right to eat that meat.

However, Paul warned them that some weak Christian may not realize that an idol is nothing. When he eats that meat his conscience hurts him because he believes he is an idolator. So for his sake, and because of their love for God, Christians should refuse to eat such meat. The liberty Christ gives keeps the believer from doing anything that would harm either a weak Christian or one who is not a Christian.

A former Muslim from India, an official of a tea business, was visiting another country. When he was offered some interesting looking food he asked, "What kind of meat is in it?"

"Fresh pork and ham," his hostess replied.

"Have you any beef?"

"No, I do not."

"Have you any lamb?"

"Fish?"

"Thank you, my dear young lady, but I won't take any."

The hostess replied, "You surprise me. Are you so under law that you can't eat pork? Don't you know that a Christian is at liberty to eat any kind of meat?"

"I am at liberty to eat it," he said, "but I am also at liberty to let it alone. I was brought up a strict Muslim. My old father, nearly 80 years of age now, is still a Muslim. Every three years I go back to India to give an account of the business of which my father is really the head, and to have a visit with the folks at home. Always when I get home I know how I will be greeted. The friends will be sitting inside. My father will come to the door when the servant announces that I am there. He will say to me, 'Have those Christians taught you to eat the filthy hog meat yet?' I will answer, 'No, Father, pork has never passed my lips.' Then I can go in and have the opportunity to tell them about Christ. If I took some of your pork or ham, I couldn't talk of Christ to my father the next time I go home."*

He was doing exactly as the apostle suggested. We have liberty not to do those things that will trouble other people. Our liberty is controlled by our love for God.

4. LIBERTY RESULTS IN SERVICE
Galatians 5:13b

Show Illustration #4

For the Apostle Paul, Christian liberty meant spending his life in service, following the example of the Lord Jesus Christ. He preached the Gospel in cities, on the seashore, and to his guards and others in jails. Once, in the earthquake-ruined Philippian prison, he told his jailor, "Believe on the Lord Jesus Christ and you will be saved." (See Acts 16:31.)

At another time when Paul was in a jail in Rome, he led Onesimus, a runaway slave, to the Saviour. Onesimus proved to be a great help to Paul. So Paul would have been glad to have him stay nearby. (See Philemon 1:13.) Instead he instructed the young man to return to his master, Philemon. He even wrote a letter to Philemon urging him to accept the disobedient slave. Paul was a great preacher and a tremendous missionary. But he never felt too important to teach the most insignificant person, even a poor slave.

Your service for God will not be exactly like the Apostle Paul's, but you do have the same liberty he had. That liberty will cause you to serve the Lord by serving others. Think of some people whom you could help this coming week. What could you do for them? You might be able to give the Gospel to certain ones. Others may be weak Christians who need your encouragement for a particular problem. Or perhaps some Christians you know are having difficulties. What could you do that would bring blessing to them?

List the days of the week in your notebook and the name of one person beside each day. Then write something you could do for each one. After you make your list, we will pray together that God will help you to use your liberty to serve Him each day this week.

(*Teacher:* Give your students time to make their lists. They may need your help or the help of classmates to think of those whom they can serve.)

---

* As told by Dr. Harry Ironside in his fine book on First Corinthians, published by Loizeaux Brothers.

Lesson 2
THE HOLY SPIRIT AND LIBERTY

NOTE TO THE TEACHER

Think of your teaching as a building process. Each brick of truth is built upon the previous brick of truth. Higher and higher the wall of learning grows. But we must be careful builders. In teaching, we need to keep checking back to the first-laid bricks of truth to make certain that they're securely in place. If the truths are half forgotten and hazy, they're like bricks which have become loose. We'll need to take time for repairs. This is review. We can build a strong wall of learning if each brick of truth is securely fastened with understanding.

It has been proved that we learn and retain much more by telling and doing than merely by hearing. To make certain that your students understand and remember the truths you are teaching, take time for questions and answers. Allow the students to tell in their own words what they have learned. Then encourage them to practice daily the truths taught, so they will be doing what they have been hearing. Give them opportunity to share with the class the changes that are taking place in their lives. The results of your teaching should show in changed lives.

Before introducing this second lesson, give your students time to discuss how they used their Christian liberty to serve the Lord during the past week.

Scripture to be studied: Galatians 5:16-21

The *aim* of the lesson: To show that when we truly walk in the Spirit, we have Christian liberty.

What your students should *know*: The Holy Spirit lives within the Christian. If we obey Him, if we let Him control us and lead us, we will not "fulfil the lust of the flesh."

What your students should *feel*: A keen desire to yield completely to the Spirit.

What your students should *do*: Confess any known sin immediately to God, so they may enjoy true Christian liberty.

Lesson outline (for teacher's and students' notebooks):
1. Obedience to the Spirit means liberty (Galatians 5:16).
2. Struggle of two natures (Galatians 5:17; Romans 7:15-25).
3. Spirit-led living is liberty (Galatians 5:18; 2 Corinthians 3:17).
4. No liberty for the one who practices sin (Galatians 5:19-21).

The verse to be memorized:

Walk in the Spirit, and ye shall not fulfil the lust of the flesh. (Galatians 5:16)

THE LESSON

Any person who truly believes in the Lord Jesus Christ has everlasting life. (See for example, John 3:16, 36; 5:24; Acts 16:31; Romans 10:9-10.) Unfortunately, many are confused as the Galatians were. They feel there are certain things they either must do or must not do in order to hold on to their salvation. They work hard trying to follow rules and laws and get all tied up like slaves. Instead, God wants them to enjoy His freedom.

1. OBEDIENCE TO THE SPIRIT MEANS LIBERTY
Galatians 5:16

If the Apostle Paul could talk today to such people, he would tell them exactly what he told the Galatians: "Walk in the Spirit. Then you will not please your old sinful selves." (See Galatians 5:16.) That is, if we who are Christians obey the Holy Spirit who lives in us, we will not do foolish things like working to earn or keep our salvation. (See Galatians 3:3.) Nor will we practice other sinful things if we are obedient to the Holy Spirit.

There are many people mentioned in the Bible who, by example, show what it means to obey God's Holy Spirit. Philip is one of those. He was quick to follow the command which the Lord Jesus had given shortly before He ascended to Heaven: "Be witnesses unto Me both in Jerusalem, and in all Judea, and in Samaria, and unto the uttermost part of the earth" (Acts 1:8). Philip went to Samaria, an area which Jews tried to avoid. Multitudes of Samaritans listened to the message of Christ that Philip preached, and many believed and were baptized. (See Acts 8:5-25.)

When two of the apostles, Peter and John, heard about the converts in Samaria, they joined Philip to help in the work. Together they preached the Gospel in many Samaritan villages.

Show Illustration #5

Just when things seemed to be at their best in Samaria, the Lord spoke to Philip through an angel. He said, "Get up and go south. Take the road which goes from Jerusalem to Gaza."

Philip might have argued with the Lord. Many, many people were coming to Christ in Samaria. Why should he leave the villages and go down to a caravan road?

However, without hesitating for a moment, Philip got up and went. There he saw an Ethiopian man riding in a chariot, reading. When the Holy Spirit said to Philip, "Go get on that chariot," Philip ran to obey. As he got near, he heard the man reading from the book of the Prophet Isaiah.

Philip called, "Do you understand what you are reading?"

"How can I unless someone teaches me?" the man replied. "Will you come up and sit beside me?" That's exactly what Philip did.

Using the same verses which the man had been reading (Isaiah 53:7-8), Philip told the Ethiopian about Jesus, the Lamb of God, who died for the sins of the world. When Philip was finished the man asked if he could be baptized.

Philip answered, "If you believe with all your heart, you may."

"I believe that Jesus Christ is the Son of God," the Ethiopian declared. After he was baptized, he went on his way full of joy.

Philip, led by the Spirit of God, went to several cities and preached the Gospel. (See Acts 8:5-8, 40.) Wherever he went, whether to a lonely rider in deserted country, or in a crowded city, he used his liberty to tell about the Lord Jesus Christ. He had that liberty because he obeyed the Holy Spirit.

2. STRUGGLE OF TWO NATURES
Galatians 5:17; Romans 7: 15-25

Christians are not always willing to obey the Spirit of God. Even Paul himself had that experience. (See Romans 7:15-25.) So he warned the Galatians (and us): "Our old selves want to do things which are against what the Holy Spirit wants. The Holy Spirit does not agree with our old sinful selves. These two are against each other. So you may not do what you want to do." (See Galatians 5:17.)

When you place your trust in Christ, God does not take away your old nature. You were born with that nature and you will have it all through your life. At the time you are born again, God gives you a new nature, a nature like that of His Son. His nature lives inside you, right alongside your old sinful nature. The two will always be together until you die.

Show Illustration #6
Inside each Christian is a constant struggle between the new nature and the old sinful nature. Each is seeking to control the child of God. Your old sinful self wants you to have your own way. Your new spiritual nature wants you to do what pleases God. Your old nature prompts you to say something unkind about someone else. Right away you say that unkind thing. "What difference does it make, anyway?" you say. Your new nature prompts you to fight back and say, "It makes a difference to God. Now that I belong to Him, I should do what He wants."

So your old self nature battles with your new spiritual nature. When you let your old self control you, you want to do wrong. When you allow the Holy Spirit to control you, you want to do right. Whenever your old sinful nature wins the battle, you have no liberty at all, no freedom to serve God, no joy, no peace, no happiness. And you yourself are responsible. You refused to let the Holy Spirit control your heart, your mind, your will. Because the Holy Spirit never leaves you (see Ephesians 4:30) and because your old sinful nature is ever with you, there will always be a struggle inside you. The Holy Spirit will control your life only if you let Him do so.

3. SPIRIT-LED LIVING IS LIBERTY
Galatians 5:18; 2 Corinthians 3:17

When the Holy Spirit is in control, you will not be defeated. If He is controlling you, He will also lead you. When He leads you, you won't be troubled with Jewish laws and rules. (See Galatians 5:18.) Nor will you do the sinful things your old nature wants you to do. Instead, you'll be free to follow His leading.

Ananias was a man who followed the leading of God's Spirit. He lived in the city of Damascus at the time Paul was saved. He knew that Paul had been responsible for putting some Christians in jail and killing others. So when the Lord told him to take a message to Paul, Ananias was afraid. He said, "Lord, I have heard many people tell about this man and how much he has harmed Your people in Jerusalem. I have also heard that he now has permission from the chief priests to make prisoners of all the Christians here in Damascus."

"Go to him," the Lord said, "for I have chosen to use him in a special way."

Show Illustration #7
The Holy Spirit led Ananias right to Paul (who was then using his name Saul). He put his hands on him, saying, "Brother Saul, the Lord Jesus who appeared to you has sent me that you might receive your sight and be filled with the Holy Spirit."

From that moment on, Paul became a most unusual servant of God. If Ananias could be here today, I believe he would say to us, "Never be afraid to allow the Holy Spirit of God to lead you. When He leads, you have true liberty." (See 2 Corinthians 3:17.)

We have Christian liberty when we obey the Spirit of God, when we allow Him to control our natures, when we follow His leading. In doing so, we are obeying the command which is part of our memory verse: "Walk in the Spirit." If you are one who is walking in the Spirit, you have this promise: "you will not fulfill the lust [desire] of the flesh [old nature]." (See Galatians 5:16.)

4. NO LIBERTY FOR THE ONE WHO PRACTICES SIN
Galatians 5:19-21

Your "flesh" is your sinful old self. So that you may know exactly how evil your old nature is, Paul lists some of the sins which the flesh is capable of doing. (*Teacher:* Read Galatians 5:19-21.)

Because God knows you have in your heart (as I do) the ability to do all kinds of wicked things, He names these examples as warnings.

There are certain plants which are poisonous. If you eat them, you will become ill, or perhaps even die. For your own safety you have to learn to recognize and avoid those plants. It is just so with your sinful old nature. You must recognize how really dangerous it is. That is why Paul lists the sins of the "flesh." To help you remember, we will put these sins into four groups:

1. Sins of impurity (adultery, fornication, uncleanness, lasciviousness)

Show Illustration #8A
Paul mentions first the wrong deeds which men do to women. The Lord Jesus said that a man who has wrong thoughts when he looks at a woman is guilty of impurity. (See Matthew 5:28.) God wants Christians to have pure thoughts and live pure lives. (See 1 Timothy 5:22.)

2. Sins of idolatry

Show Illustration #8B
We are warned here against the worship of false gods and against witchcraft. God does not want us to worship images of man or beast. We are not to pray to them, or to the dead, or to spirits. He wants us to trust and worship Him alone.

3. Sins of ill-nature (hatred, variance [quarrelsomeness, strife], emulations [jealousy], wrath [outburst of anger], strife [factions], seditions [divisions], heresies [false doctrine], envyings, murders)

Show Illustration #8C

Paul says your old sinful self will want to hate, fight, be jealous, argue, be angry. It will cause you and others to divide into little groups and criticize each other. Many murders have resulted from these very sins. A person may become so angry that he murders another. Others are murdered in a different way. Someone is unkind to another. Or someone is jealous of him/her. And the person dies of a broken heart. This person has actually been murdered by the unkindness or the jealousy.

4. Sins of excess

Show Illustration #8D

To get drunk when you are alone or to drink with others (revellings) is equally sinful.

Real Christians may fall into any of these or other sins. But when he/she does, the Spirit's liberty is gone. The Christian is miserable and feels wretched until his/her sin is confessed. (See 1 John 1:9.) He/she is bound like a slave by sins of the flesh, as well as by trying to keep the law.

However, if a person sins *continually*, he/she proves that he/she is not a Christian at all. That person "shall not inherit the kingdom of God" (Galatians 5:21).

Will you list in your notebook, please, the sins of which you are guilty? (No one will see your list.) Your sins may be some of those which Paul mentioned to the Galatians; you may have other sins. After your list is made, we will have a time of silent prayer. During that time, name your sin to God. He already knows the sin. But in order to confess it, you must tell Him what that sin is. Ask Him to forgive that sin. Then thank Him for doing so.

After silent prayer, we will have one after another lead us in public prayer. Ask God to help us obey His Holy Spirit. Ask Him to control and overcome our old natures. Ask Him to help us to follow the leading of His Spirit. Ask Him to forgive our sins so we may enjoy the liberty He wants us to have.

Lesson 3
LIBERTY FOR SPIRITUAL LIVING

NOTE TO THE TEACHER

The Holy Spirit forms spiritual character in the Christian who is yielded to Him. That character is best described by the nine-fold fruit of the Spirit mentioned in Galatians 5:22-23. Taken together, these characteristics present a portrait of our Lord.

We should prayerfully examine ourselves in relation to this lesson. Our students are studying our lives. Do we present an illustration of Christ? We have these qualities only if we have a vital union with Christ and are yielded to His Spirit.

Under point three in our outline (Sowing to the flesh), there are many Bible examples of those who sowed to the flesh. In this lesson we have referred to Abraham because Paul spoke of him in Galatians. You may want to mention the reaping of Adam and Eve as mentioned in Genesis 3:16-19. Jonah sowed disobedience when he refused to go to Nineveh. He reaped a raging sea storm; being tossed into the sea; and finally, being swallowed by a great fish in which he spent three days and three nights.

Perhaps David's life is one of the most terrifying Bible accounts of sowing and reaping. If you are teaching young people and adults, you should tell the events recorded in 2 Samuel 11:1-18. While King David's men were off to battle, David was at home. When he saw Bathsheba bathing, he should have turned away. Instead, he lusted after her and shortly committed adultery with her. Then he schemed, trying to cover his sin. (See 2 Samuel 11:6-13.)

He called Bathsheba's husband, Uriah, back from battle and encouraged him to go home to his wife. That way it would appear that the child she was to have would be Uriah's. But Uriah refused to go in to her because he was so loyal to his country and fellow soldiers. Then David plotted the murder of Uriah. (See 2 Samuel 11:14-21.)

Adultery, scheming and murder were all parts of David's sowing. No wonder he cried, "Have mercy upon me. O God . . . my sin is ever before me." That confession and the rest of Psalm 51 were written as a result of his sin with Bathsheba.

Despite his confession, David reaped what he sowed: one of his sons also committed adultery with his half-sister, David's daughter (2 Samuel 13:1-15); hatred took over David's family (2 Samuel 13:22); he lost the hearts of the people of his kingdom (2 Samuel 15:6); the baby born to Bathsheba died and two of his sons were murdered (2 Samuel 12:15-19; 13:23-33; 18:9-17). David reaped 14 years of heartbreak for his sin. Like him, we reap what we sow. That is a law which cannot be broken, even for the Christian.

Scripture to be studied: Galatians 5:22-26; 6:7-9

The *aim* of the lesson: To show that Spirit-controlled living yields a good harvest in this life and in Heaven.

What your students should *know*: God wants the fruit of the Spirit to flourish in our lives.

What your students should *feel*: A hatred and a dread of allowing our old sinful selves to control us; a love and desire to live out our new spiritual natures.

What your students should *do*: Ask the Lord to show them how He can live through them during the coming week.

Lesson outline (for the teacher's and students' notebooks):

1. The fruit of the Spirit (Galatians 5:22-23).
2. Living by the Spirit (Galatians 5:24-26).
3. Sowing to the flesh (Galatians 6:7-8a).
4. Sowing to the Spirit (Galatians 6:8b-9).

The verse to be memorized:

Walk in the Spirit, and ye shall not fulfil the lust of the flesh. (Galatians 5:16)

THE LESSON

Let us imagine that we are walking down a path which we have never been on before. Look! There in the distance is a large tree. Keep watching it and as we get closer tell me what kind of tree it is. Suppose the tree has leaves like a cherry tree. (*Teacher:* Name a fruit-bearing tree familiar to your class.) The bark is rough and dark like cherry wood. The tree is covered with clusters of dark, ripe cherries.

Would you think it safe to say that the tree really is a cherry tree? What would you think if I were to say, "I do not believe this is a cherry tree; it's a pear tree"?

I might have mistaken the shape of the leaves or the color and texture of the bark. But the fruit will tell which it is, for surely I would not mistake a cherry for a pear. The two fruits are of different size, color and shape, and entirely different in taste. If the tree were bearing cherries, it would have to be a cherry tree. The fruit is the final proof.

The Lord Jesus once said, "Every tree is known by its fruit. A good tree does not give bad fruit, and a bad tree does not give good fruit . . . . You do not gather figs or grapes from a bramble bush." (See Luke 6:43-45.). Just so, a person is known by the life he/she lives. If the person belongs to God's family, his/her life should show what God is like. That one should not show impatience or jealousy or any other wrong attitude.

At another time Jesus explained how our lives may show that we belong to Him. He said, "I am the true vine . . . . Abide in Me, and I in you. As the branch cannot bear fruit of itself, except it abide in the vine; no more can you, except you abide in Me. I am the vine, you are the branches." (See John 15:1-5.)

Fruit grows from the branches and gets nourishment from them. The branches get nourishment from the tree. So it is that believers who abide in Christ and allow His life to flow through them, produce the fruit of His nature.

Jesus said, "You will praise [glorify] My Father if you bear much fruit." (See John 15:8.)

1. THE FRUIT OF THE SPIRIT
Galatians 5:22-23

Perhaps you are wondering what kind of "fruit" Jesus meant. Paul gives an explanation in his letter to the Galatians. (*Teacher:* Have class read Galatians 5:22-23.) Here is a list of nine qualities which every believer has if he/she is letting the Holy Spirit control him completely.

Show Illustration #9

(*Teacher:* Print in each grape the name of one characteristic as you mention it. If your students are not acquainted with grapes, you will have to explain that this is the fruit of the vine to which the Lord Jesus referred in John 15.)

The first three qualities–love, joy, peace–refer to thinking habits. You think loving, joyful thoughts and have peace of mind when you allow God's Spirit to control you. This kind of love leads you to do unselfish things for others, without expecting something in return. (See 1 Corinthians 13.) Joy keeps you thanking God for everything that comes into your life. (See Romans 14:17; 2 Corinthians 6:4-10; 1 Thessalonians 1:6.) Peace is quietness inside. (See Philippians 4:7.)

The next three qualities–longsuffering, gentleness, goodness–affect the way you act toward others. Longsuffering causes you to be patient even when people treat you with meanness. Gentleness makes you kind to others. Goodness makes you ready to do good.

The last three qualities–faithfulness, meekness, self-control–guide your daily conduct. Faithfulness will make you dependable in whatever you do. Meekness will keep you in the background instead of showing off. Self-control will keep your desires in check.

There is One who is the perfect example of this fruit, the Lord Jesus. (*Teacher:* You may want to refer to His days just before and during His trials and crucifixion. These characteristics were especially evident at that time because of the awful experiences He endured.) Jesus could say, "I do always those things that please My Father." (See John 8:29.) Can you say that? Like every Christian, you have the liberty to yield yourself to God each day. As you do, you will have the fruit of His Spirit.

2. LIVING BY THE SPIRIT
Galatians 5:24-26

To the Galatians (and us) Paul says that those who belong to Christ Jesus should live as if they had died to the desires of their old natures. (See Galatians 5:24; Romans 6:6, 11.)

As far as God is concerned, the day you accepted Christ as Saviour, you died with Christ. (See Romans 6:8; Galatians 2:20.)

Show Illustration #10

When your old sinful self (your flesh) wants to sin, you must remind yourself that you are dead to sin. (See Romans 6:11-14; Galatians 6:14.) Since you live by the Spirit of God, you walk in step with Him. (See Galatians 5:25.) If you keep giving yourself to Him, He will give the power you need to keep from sinning. So your new spiritual nature will be victor over your old sinful nature.

3. SOWING TO THE FLESH
Galatians 6:7-8a

Paul again speaks of the old sinful nature and the new spiritual nature in Galatians 6:7-9. (*Teacher:* Read these verses to your students.) When you sow seed, you reap a harvest. If you plant corn, you reap corn. You do not get corn if you plant rice. This is God's law. It never changes. Every day you're sowing either fleshly acts of your old sinful nature or spiritual acts of your new Christian nature. If you sow fleshly acts, you reap sinful things. If you sow acts of your new nature you reap spiritual things.

Abraham (of whom Paul spoke in Galatians 4) obeyed his old sinful nature. He became impatient because God did not give him a son by the time he thought he should have a son. Further, Abraham doubted that God was going to keep His promise of giving him a son. So he took things into his own hands and had a son by a slave woman, Hagar. That son's name was Ishmael.

Later God gave Abraham the promised son, Isaac, by his wife, Sarah. Ishmael hated his young brother Isaac. (See Genesis 21:9.) So even though Abraham loved both sons, he had to send Ishmael to another land. He sowed impatience and a lack of trust in God. He reaped separation from his older son.

Show Illustration #11

From Ishmael, off in the land of Arabia, came uncounted thousands of Arabs. They continue to be born even today. From Isaac, the son promised by God, have come unnumbered thousands of Israelites. Now, thousands of years since Ishmael and Isaac were born, the Arabic descendants (of Ishmael) and the Israelite descendants (of Isaac) war against each other. Like most harvests, Abraham reaped more than he sowed!

God cannot be fooled. If you sow the deeds of your old sinful self, you will reap the full results of your sin.

4. SOWING TO THE SPIRIT
Galatians 6:8b-9

Like every Christian, you have liberty to "sow to the Spirit" (Galatians 6:8b). That is, you're free to do the things which please the Spirit of God. That sowing will also result in a harvest. You may reap good things in this life. Or you may have to wait until you stand before the Judgment Seat of Christ to reap your harvest. That harvest will last eternally. (See 2 Corinthians 5:10; Matthew 16:27; Revelation 22:12.)

Show Illustration #12

Paul looked forward to the day when he would receive his rewards. Like many other Christians, he will receive a crown because he looked for the coming of the Lord Jesus. (See 2 Timothy 4:8.) For preaching the Gospel willingly, for winning souls to Christ, he will have rewards. (See 1 Corinthians 9:17; 1 Thessalonians 2:19.) Christians are promised other rewards, too: for enduring trial (James 1:12); for being a good Christian example to others (1 Peter 5:2-4); for rejoicing even though you may have been treated cruelly or lied about (Matthew 5:12); for loving your enemies and doing good to them (Luke 6:35). There is even a reward for the one who gives a cup of water to another Christian (Mark 9:41). These are only a few of the rewards mentioned in the Bible.

Right now, will you silently ask God to fill your heart with His love, joy, peace, longsuffering, gentleness, goodness, faith, meekness, temperance? Ask Him to show you how He wants to use you this week. (*Teacher:* Allow time for silent prayer.)

If you feel that you already know some ways God wants to use you, will you list them in your notebook, please? Then we'll pray for each other.

Lesson 4
THE LAW OF CHRIST *

Scripture to be studied: Galatians 6 and all the references in the lesson material.

The *aim* of the lesson: To show that by obeying the law of Christ, believers become Christlike.

What your students should *know*: The standards of the Law of Moses are not high enough for Christians. God has given us the perfect law of Christ which we are to obey because we want to.

What your students should *feel*: A determination to obey the law of Christ gladly.

What your students should *do*: Trust the Holy Spirit to help them obey the commands, the rules, and the guides of the law of Christ.

Lesson outline (for the teacher's and students' notebooks):
1. Instructions included in the law of Christ.
2. Guides for living under the law of Christ.
3. The power of the law of Christ.
4. The purpose of the law of Christ.

The verse to be memorized:

Walk in the Spirit, and ye shall not fulfil the lust of the flesh. (Galatians 5:16)

NOTE TO THE TEACHER

In this series, we have been studying that the Christian has liberty to choose to do that which pleases God. In today's lesson we learn that we please God by obeying the law of Christ.

As in all of Paul's books, he concludes Galatians by telling exactly how to live the Christian life. He refers to the law of Christ and mentions a few principles to be followed (Galatians 6:1-10). We have used Dr. Ryrie's excellent material to help you to enlarge on the text.

*The material in this lesson has been adapted from a section of the book entitled *The Grace of God* by Dr. Charles C. Ryrie. Copyright 1963, Moody Press, Moody Bible Institute of Chicago, IL. Used by permission. Every teacher should have this splendid book.

THE LESSON

We have learned that the law which God gave to His people, the Israelites, was not for the Galatians nor is it for us today. Keeping that law will not help us to earn our salvation or to hold on to our salvation. Does that mean, then, that there are no rules or laws for Christians? Can they live as they please? Listen carefully to today's lesson.

The law which God gave through Moses to His people was severe. Nevertheless, it was a good law and it was fair. (See Exodus 19:5-6.) It said that if a man wanted to be blessed, he had to obey the commands. He had to offer sacrifices for his sins, he had to keep certain days holy, he had to follow Jewish ceremonies, he had to worship in a certain way. If he did not obey the law, he was punished, often by death. So it was a case of do or die!

The Galatians had not understood that the law was given to Israel and Israel only. (See Leviticus 26:46.) They didn't realize that with the death of Christ the old law was changed. (See Hebrews 7:12; 2 Corinthians 3:7-11.) The old law had its use–it showed people that they were sinners. (See Romans 3:20; 1 Timothy 1:9-10.) It pointed the unsaved to Christ. (See Galatians 3:19-25.) But it could never save anyone. (See Acts 13:39.)

The standards of the old law were good, but they were not high enough. For instance, the Galatians might have kept the old law which said, "You shall not take the name of the Lord your God in vain." But they could have lost their tempers, saying harsh things to others. In Galatians we are told that there is a new law. This new law says, "Let your speech be always with grace, seasoned with salt" (Colossians 4:6a). This covers everything a person says. The old law required a person to love his neighbor as himself. (See Leviticus 19:18.) The new law commands us to love others *as Christ loved us*. (See John 13:34.)

Instead of obeying the old law in order to get blessed, we are to obey the new law because we have been blessed. We obey because we want to, not because we are afraid not to.

Paul speaks of this new law as "the law of Christ." (See Galatians 6:2.) It is also spoken of as the "perfect law of liberty" (James 1:25) and "the law of the Spirit of life" (Romans 8:2).

The law of Christ is a set of rules and guides for the Christian today. It is that law which we Christians are to obey.

1. INSTRUCTIONS INCLUDED IN THE LAW OF CHRIST

The law of Christ contains hundreds of specific commandments. Some are commands to do certain things. Others tell us what not to do. Rules made by our Christian leaders are also included in the law of Christ.

1. What to do

If we know a person who is doing something sinful, we are commanded to lead him/her back into the right way. (See Galatians 6:1.) This we must do humbly ("in the spirit of meekness"). This is a command to be obeyed.

Show Illustration #13A

We are commanded to help those who have problems or troubles. When we share their burdens, it takes some of the load off of them. (See Galatians 6:2.) This is part of the law of Christ.

(*Teacher:* There are many other positive commands. You may want to have your students read some of them. For example: Romans 12:1; 13:1; 1 Corinthians 11:28; 2 Corinthians 6:17; Galatians 6:6, 9, 10; Ephesians 5:22; Colossians 4:6; 1 Thessalonians 5:16-18; 2 Thessalonians 3:13; 1 Timothy 2:8; 2 Timothy 4:2; Titus 2:7-8; Hebrews 10:24; James 1:5; 1 Peter 2:21; 2 Peter 3:18; 1 John 2:6; 2 John 8; 3 John 11a; Revelation 2:5.)

2. What not to do

The law of Christ also includes certain things which Christians are told not to do.

Show Illustration #13B

We are not to lose heart (or turn cowards) when we do good. For example, suppose you tell someone about the Lord Jesus Christ and he/she laughs at you and may even tell you that you are a fool. If you are obeying the law of Christ, you will not get discouraged. Nor will you become a coward. (See Galatians 6:9.)

(*Teacher:* You may want to share with your students examples of some other negative commands: Romans 12:2a; 2 Corinthians 6:14; Ephesians 4:30; Philippians 2:4; Colossians 3:21; 1 Thessalonians 5:19; 2 Thessalonians 3:14; 1 Timothy 4:7; 2 Timothy 1:8; Titus 2:10; Hebrews 10:25; James 4:11; 1 Peter 3:9; 2 Peter 3:8; 1 John 4:l; 2 John 10; 3 John 11.)

3. Rules

As we have seen, the law of Christ contains things we are to do and things we are not to do, as recorded in the New Testament. It also includes rules which are made by our Christian leaders. God has given authority to Christian leaders who guide us. (See Ephesians 4:11-12; 1 Timothy 3:15; Hebrews 13:7, 17.)

Show Illustration #13C

We are to obey joyfully the rules which our Christian leaders make. (See Hebrews 13:17.) This is an important part of the law of Christ.

2. GUIDES FOR LIVING UNDER THE LAW OF CHRIST

The commands and rules do not cover every part of our Christian conduct. So, in addition, God has given us guides that will help us in our everyday living.

1. Is it a weight?

Show Illustration #14A

We are told to put aside anything that is a weight and any sin which might trip us. (See Hebrews 12:1.) The Christian life is like a race. A runner who insists on carrying a heavy load won't win the race. So it is with the Christian. If there is anything in his/her life keeping him/her from being his/her best for God, it is a weight. Whatever that weight is, the person must get rid of it, according to the law of Christ. (*Teacher:* Mention some definite "weights" which your class might have.)

2. Is it a habit?

We are to test ourselves to see if we have habits which are ruling us. "I am allowed to do all things, but all things are not good for me to do. Even though I am free to do all things, I will not do them if it would be hard for me to stop." (See 1 Corinthians 6:12.) This was Paul's guide and it should be ours.

Show Illustration #14B

Do you have a habit that controls you? It may be any number of things: smoking, chewing gum, talking too much. Anything that has power over you is a habit. You may not see any harm in that thing. But what good does it do? You are to control your habits; your habits are not to control you. This is a guide for living under the law of Christ.

Because weights and habits are harmful to us, God wants us to get rid of them.

3. Is it a stumbling stone?

Show Illustration #14C

Some things which may appear to be quite all right for us to do. But if other Christians (or non-Christians) see us do those things and they are troubled, we must not do them. If we do, we cause them to stumble.

In Corinth, some of the Christians ate meat which had been offered to idols. They knew that an idol is nothing, so the meat offered to it was offered to nothing. So they felt there was no harm in eating that meat. This bothered the Corinthians. So Paul told the Christians that although they had liberty to eat that meat, their love for others should keep them from doing so. (See 1 Corinthians 8:1-13.) This is a guide for us who are living under the law of Christ. We should not do anything that causes weaker ones to stumble. We avoid doing that thing because of our love for others.

4. Does it display God?

Show Illustration #14D

Whatever we do is to be done to the glory of God. (See 1 Corinthians 10:31.) Can I ask God to bless the thing I am doing? Does it show others what God is like? Does it help others to turn to God? Doing everything "to the glory of God," showing God off, is a guide for those of us who are obeying the law of Christ.

3. THE POWER OF THE LAW OF CHRIST

The commands and rules and guides for living under the law of Christ are perfect. If we are going to obey them, we must have more power than we ourselves have. Happily, God who gave the law of Christ, has also provided the power to obey it. That power is the Holy Spirit who lives within each Christian from the moment he/she is born again. (See John 14:17; Romans 8:9; 1 Corinthians 6:19.)

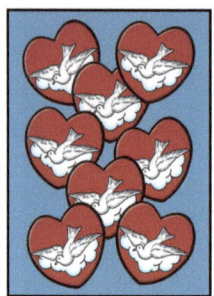

Show Illustration #15

At the time of the baptism of the Lord Jesus, the Holy Spirit, like a dove, came down on Him. Because the Holy Spirit is a spirit, He cannot be seen. However, to help us remember that He is in the heart of every believer, we have pictured many hearts, each with a dove inside. The Holy Spirit living inside you will make you able to obey the law of Christ, if you will trust Him and follow Him completely.

4. THE PURPOSE OF THE LAW OF CHRIST

By obeying the law of Christ, believers become like Him. This is the purpose of the law of Christ.

If we are to be like Christ, we'll have to follow His example:

Show Illustration #16A

1. He was tender-hearted (compassionate) toward others. Even when crowds of people thronged Him, He was never impatient. He was as tender to them as a father is to his children. (See Matthew 9:36; 14:14; 15:32; Mark 6:34; 8:2.)

Show Illustration #16B

2. He loved people with all His heart, even those who turned their backs on Him. That is why He wept over them when He looked at the city. (See Mark 10:21-22; Luke 19:41.)

Show Illustration #16C

3. He offered to help people, even before being asked. (See Mark 8:7; John 5:6.) He healed the lame and others. While we aren't able to do that, we can certainly be helpful in other ways.

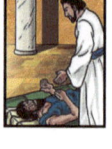

Show Illustration #16D

4. He searched for people in order to give them God's message. (See Matthew 9:35; 15:10; Mark 4:1; 6:2.)

By obeying the commands and rules and guides of the law of Christ, we will become like Christ. However, we will never be like Him in public until we practice in private what He did.

Show Memory Verse Poster

5. He knew and used the Word of God. (See Matthew 4:4.)

6. He constantly spent time with His Father in prayer. (See Matthew 14:23; Mark 1:35; Luke 5:16; 6:12; 9:18, 29; 11:1.)

This is the pattern which the Christian should follow. By so doing, you will be walking in the Spirit and not fulfilling the lust of the flesh.

If you are an earnest Christian, you want to be like Christ. You want to glorify God. You want to show Him off to the world. God has doubtless spoken to you today, showing you some command, some rule, some guide He wants you to obey. Will you write it (or them) in your notebook?

Then ask Him to help you to obey Him gladly.

www.ingramcontent.com/pod-product-compliance
Lightning Source LLC
Chambersburg PA
CBHW060804090426
42736CB00002B/155